THIS BOOK BELONGS TO:

_____

WELCOME TO MISSOURI

Dedicated to all the explorers.

ISBN 978-1-958985-78-6

www.joeysavestheday.com

A Mimi Book

Missouri was named after the Missouria tribe, whose name means "people of the big canoes." French explorers wrote the name on maps in the 1600s, and it later became the name of both the Missouri River and the state.

Missouri was the twenty-fourth state to join the Union. It officially joined on August 10, 1821.

24th

Missouri is located in the Midwestern region of the United States and is bordered by eight states: Iowa, Nebraska, Kansas, Oklahoma, Arkansas, Tennessee, Kentucky, and Illinois.

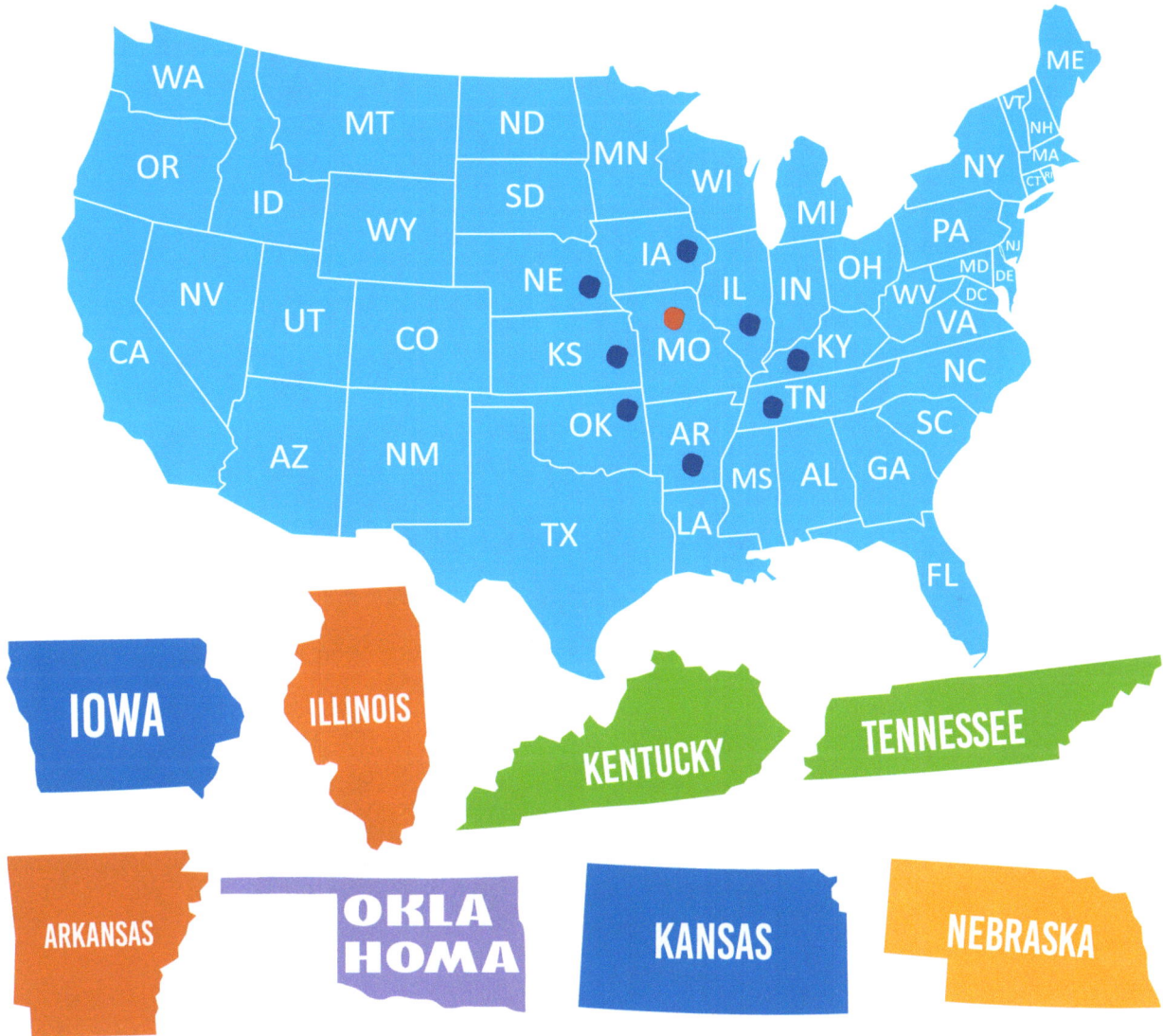

Jefferson City is the capital of Missouri.
It officially became the capital in 1821.

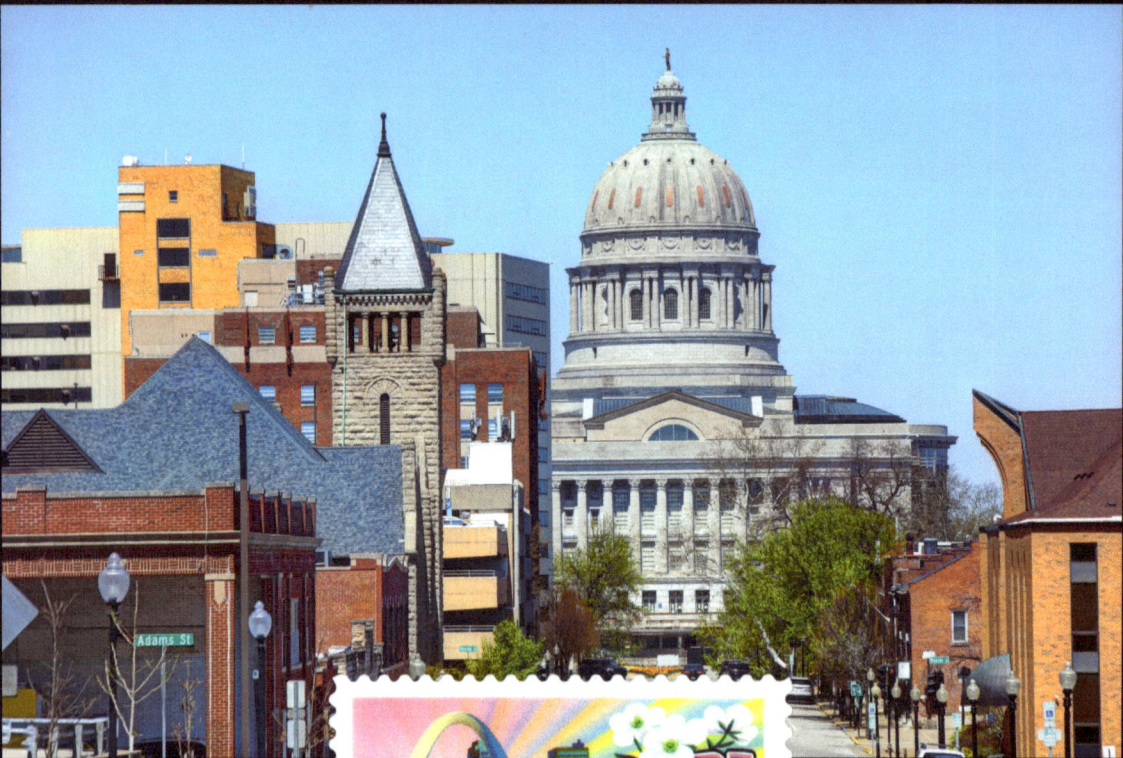

Missouri

Jefferson City, Missouri, has an estimated population of about 42,560 people.

Missouri is the twenty-first largest state in the United States by area.

Missouri

Table Rock Lake in Southwest Missouri.

There are approximately 6,282,900 people residing in the state of Missouri.

Kansas City, Missouri

George Washington Carver (1864–1943), born in Missouri, became one of America's most famous scientists. Growing up with little, he devoted his life to studying plants and helping farmers. At Tuskegee Institute, he taught crop rotation to restore soil and found hundreds of new uses for peanuts, sweet potatoes, and other crops.

Missouri is known for a delicious snack called toasted ravioli, which actually isn't toasted at all, it's fried! This fun food was created in St. Louis when a chef accidentally dropped ravioli into hot oil. The result was a crispy, golden pocket filled with warm, seasoned meat or cheese. Toasted ravioli is usually sprinkled with Parmesan cheese and served with a cup of marinara sauce for dipping.

Missouri

There are 114 counties in Missouri.

Here is a list of twenty of those counties:

Audrain	Cedar	Henry	Monroe
Bates	Cooper	Jasper	Oregon
Boone	DeKalb	Laclede	Platte
Callaway	Franklin	Macon	Scotland
Carroll	Greene	Miller	Vernon

Missouri's wetlands are soggy, wild places filled with marshes, swamps, and slow-moving water. Long ago, these wetlands covered huge areas of the state, especially in the Bootheel region. Today, only a small part remains, but they are still bursting with life. Frogs, turtles, fish, birds, and hundreds of plant species depend on these watery habitats. Wetlands also help protect people by soaking up floodwater and keeping rivers cleaner. They're some of the richest and most important natural areas in Missouri.

The Pony Express began in St. Joseph, Missouri, in 1860 and quickly became one of the most famous mail services in American history. Riders on fast horses carried letters nearly 2,000 miles west to California, helping people stay connected long before telephones or the internet existed.

The Burfordville Covered Bridge is the oldest covered bridge still standing in Missouri. Work on it began in 1858, but it wasn't finished until after the Civil War. This wooden bridge crosses the Whitewater River right beside the historic Bollinger Mill, creating one of the prettiest scenes in the state. Built with strong wooden beams and iron rods, it once carried wagons and farmers to the mill.

Forest Park is one of the largest and most beautiful city parks in the United States, right in the heart of St. Louis. It's a place where families can explore museums, stroll around sparkling lakes, and enjoy wide green spaces that feel peaceful even in the middle of a busy city. One of the prettiest spots in the park is Pagoda Circle, a round, tree-lined area with a charming pavilion that sits beside the water.

The Missouri state bird is the Eastern Bluebird. It was chosen as the state bird on March 30, 1927.

MISSOURI

The official state flower of Missouri is the White Hawthorn Blossom. It was chosen as the state flower on March 16, 1923.

A couple of Missouri's nicknames include the Show Me State and the Ozark State.

THE SHOW  ST8

And

The OHZ st8

Missouri's state motto, "Salus populi suprema lex esto," translates from Latin to "The welfare of the people is the supreme law." It was officially adopted in 1822.

MISSOURI
MISSOURI
MISSOURI
MISSOURI

The abbreviation for Missouri is MO.

MO

Missouri's state flag was officially adopted on March 22, 1913.

Some crops grown in Missouri are corn, cotton, rice, and soybeans.

Some animals that live in Missouri are beavers, bobcats, bats, coyotes, red foxes, and woodchucks.

Missouri experiences significant temperature fluctuations throughout the year. On the hottest day ever recorded, temperatures reached 118 degrees Fahrenheit in Warsaw on July 14, 1954. On the flip side, the coldest it's ever been hit a bone-chilling -40 degrees Fahrenheit in Warsaw on February 13, 1905.

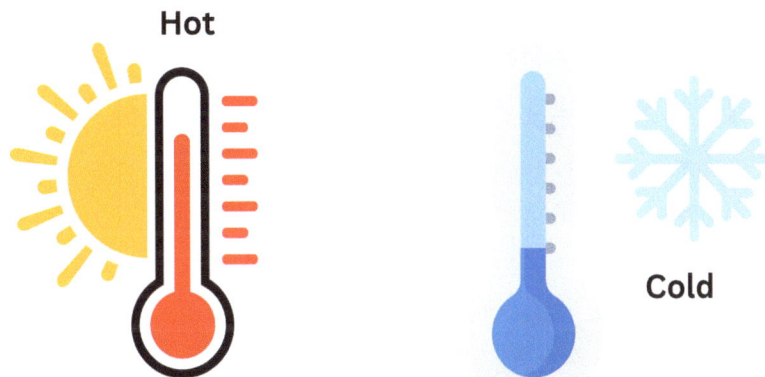

Hot

Cold

ZOO

The Saint Louis Zoo is one of the most popular zoos in the country, and it's located in Forest Park in St. Louis, Missouri. Kids can explore animals from all around the world, including lions, giraffes, zebras, penguins, sea lions, and bright tropical birds.

28

MO

Gateway Arch National Park is located in the heart of St. Louis, Missouri, and is home to the tallest monument in the United States. The shiny stainless-steel arch rises 630 feet into the sky and celebrates America's westward expansion.

AIRPORT ✈

St. Louis Lambert International Airport is the biggest and busiest airport in Missouri, located in St. Louis on the eastern side of the state. You can find it at 10701 Lambert International Boulevard, St. Louis, Missouri. This airport connects travelers to cities all across the country, with flights to places like Denver, Atlanta, Orlando, and Phoenix.

The St. Louis Cardinals are one of the most famous baseball teams in the country, and they play in St. Louis, on the eastern side of Missouri. Their home field is Busch Stadium, a bright red ballpark with a great view of the Gateway Arch. The Cardinals have a long, proud history and are known for winning many championships, making them one of the most successful teams in Major League Baseball.

FOOTBALL

The Missouri Tigers are the most well-known college football team in the state, and they play in Columbia, Missouri, right in the center of the state. Their home field is Memorial Stadium, often called "The Zou," a loud and exciting place filled with fans wearing black and gold. The Tigers compete in the Southeastern Conference, where they face some of the toughest teams in college football.

The Flowering Dogwood is Missouri's state tree. In spring, it bursts into beautiful white flowers that make the forests look like they're sprinkled with snow. During summer, its leaves turn a deep green, and in fall, the tree shows off bright red berries and colorful leaves. Even though it's not very tall, the dogwood is one of Missouri's most loved trees because it brings color and beauty to every season.

The Channel Catfish is Missouri's state fish. It has smooth skin, a long tail, and whiskers that help it feel around for food in dark or muddy water. Channel catfish live in rivers and lakes all across Missouri and can grow surprisingly big.

Can you name these?

I hope you enjoyed
learning about
Missouri.

To explore fun facts about the other 49 states,
visit my website at www.joeysavestheday.com.
You'll also find a wide variety of homeschool
resources to support joyful learning at home.
If you enjoyed this book, I would be grateful if
you left a review. Your feedback truly helps.
Thank you for your support!

TIME
TO SAY
GOODBYE

Check out these other interesting books in the 50 States Fact Books Series!

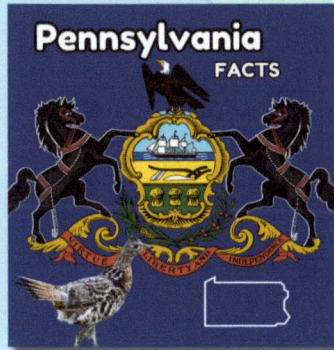

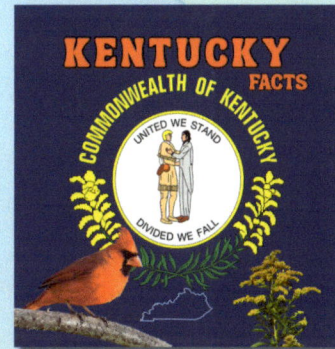

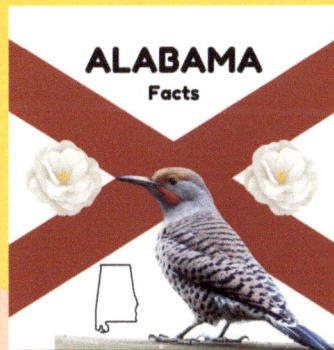

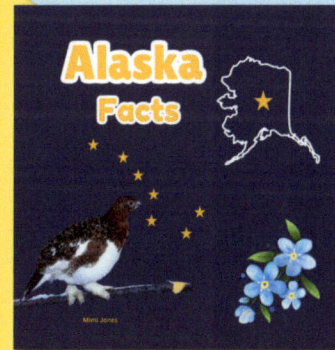

OHIO FACTS

Pennsylvania FACTS

TEXAS FACTS

KANSAS FACTS

CALIFORNIA FACTS
CALIFORNIA REPUBLIC

KENTUCKY FACTS
COMMONWEALTH OF KENTUCKY
UNITED WE STAND
DIVIDED WE FALL

GEORGIA FACTS

ALABAMA Facts

Alaska Facts

www.mimibooks.com

www.ingramcontent.com/pod-product-compliance
Lightning Source LLC
Chambersburg PA
CBHW041549040426
42447CB00002B/108